CW01460610

What Does the Lord Require?

An Examination of the Indictment of God Against His People in Micah 6:1-8

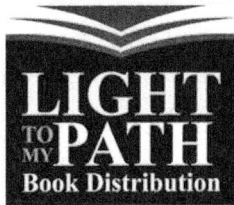

LIGHT TO MY PATH
Book Distribution

F. Wayne Mac Leod

Light To My Path Book Distribution
Sydney Mines, Nova Scotia, CANADA B1V 1Y5

What Does God Require

Copyright © 2018 by F. Wayne Mac Leod

Contents

Preface

Micah 6:1-8 exposes a people who had lost their heart for God. Despite all that God had done for them, His ways had become wearisome. They no longer understood God or His heart for them. Speaking through His servant Micah, the Lord instructs His people in His purpose for their lives.

Here in this passage, Micah reveals the false notions his people had about God and His requirements. God's people spoke of burnt offerings, rivers of oil and firstborn sacrifices. God pointed them to justice, kindness, and humility. Israel focused on religious duty and painful obligations, but God showed them the way of compassion and willing surrender.

What does God require of us? Ultimately, He demands nothing of us that He is not first willing to offer abundantly to us in His Son Jesus Christ –justice, kindness and true humility. How easy it is for us to make our faith about all the things we do for God. Micah, however, challenges us to do for others what God has already done for us.

The faith Micah presented to his people was a faith that impacted others. It was a faith that demonstrated in word and deeds the justice, kindness and compassion of God to a world in need. May the Lord renew Micah's message in our day through this simple study.

God bless,

F. Wayne Mac Leod

Chapter 1 - An Indictment Against God's People

The setting is a court. Standing before us is the Creator of the heavens and the earth. He is the One against whom a serious offence has been committed. As the court session begins, the accusation is declared:

> *(3) "O my people, what have I done to you? How have I wearied you? Answer me! – Micah 6:3 ESV*

Notice the words, "O my people." These words reveal the identity of the other party in this case. The case is between God and His people.

The remaining words of verse 3 declare the reason for the trial. In His opening sentence, God asks two questions:

1) What have I done to you?
2) How have I wearied you?

These questions are directed to the people of God. They had turned their back on Him and found His demands to be a burden. They lusted after other gods and spurned His Law. Like a husband and wife, however, they had been joined by a legally binding covenant promise. That covenant stated that God would be their God, and they would be His people. This oath of faithfulness bound them to each other.

As the allegation is declared, we meet the jury. This jury consists of the mountains, hills and the foundations of the earth. They are called to hear the charge of God against His people:

> *(1) Hear what the LORD says: Arise, plead your case before the mountains, and let the hills hear your voice. (2) Hear, you mountains, the indictment of the LORD, and you enduring foundations of the earth, for the LORD has an indictment against his people, and he will contend with Israel. – Micah 6:1-2 ESV*

The mountains, hills, and earth's foundation existed from the beginning of creation and witnessed history's unfolding. They saw the work of God from the start. They could testify to His character, power and efforts. They understood the big picture. Who could question the ancient wisdom of the mountains and hills?

As the case continues, God reminded His people of what He had done for them. He begins by recalling how He had rescued them from the cruel slavery of Egypt:

> *(4) For I brought you up from the land of Egypt and redeemed you from the house of slavery, and I sent before you Moses, Aaron, and Miriam. – Micah 6:4 ESV*

As they travelled through the wilderness toward the Promised Land, Israel encountered the opposition of King Balak of Moab, who wanted to curse them. Balak hired a false prophet by the name of Balaam to bring this curse upon the people of God.

> *(5) O my people, remember what Balak king of Moab devised, and what Balaam the son of Beor answered him – Micah 6:5a ESV*

God met with the prophet Balaam, however, and kept him from cursing His people. He protected His people lest their enemy harm them. This was only one of many incidents that illustrated God's care and protection in the wilderness.

Finally, God pointed his children to the events that took place from Shittim to Gilgal.

and what happened from Shittim to Gilgal, that you may know the righteous acts of the LORD." - Micah 6:5b ESV

Israel was living in the region of Shittim at the time of Balaam. After averting the curse of Balak, it was here that they fell into the sin of immorality and idolatry (Numbers 25:1). From this city, Joshua sent the first spies into the Promised Land (Joshua 2:1).

According to Joshua 4:19, Gilgal was the first camp of Israel in the Promised Land. In Gilgal, Joshua circumcised all the men who had travelled through the wilderness (Joshua 5:8-9). The first Passover celebration in the Promised Land took place in Gilgal, and it was at Gilgal, the Lord's daily provision of manna stopped (Joshua 4:10-12). This city would be Israel's base as they conquered the Canaanite nations and settled into the land (Joshua 10:7-8). By pointing His people to what took place from Shittim to Gilgal, the Lord reminded His people of how He protected them from the days of Baalam until they took possession of the Promised Land.

The Lord presented His evidence. He revealed how He cared for and delivered His people from their cruel bondage in Egypt. As they wandered in the wilderness, He protected them, gave them overwhelming victory, and settled them into their land. Admittedly, life was not all ease and comfort for Israel, but God had always been faithful.

What Does God Require?

The temptation of Israel was to look at the struggle of the moment. She saw the enemy and felt God had abandoned her. She ate manna for the seventh time in the week and felt rejected because God did not give her more variety in her diet. Instead of seeing the provision and protection of God, she grumbled and complained. Looking back over time, however, Israel would see the hand of God giving victory over every enemy attack. She would also marvel at the love of a God who, faithfully without fault, provided manna every day for forty years to sustain them.

While God's ways were different from her ways, He had always been faithful to Israel. He has a purpose for what He does. His objective is not just to make us comfortable but to train us in godliness and draw us closer to Himself. This training requires that we be stretched at times. While God may not always make our life comfortable, He will certainly make us better people through the experiences He sends our way.

Before concluding, let me take a moment to examine the question, "How have I wearied you?" This question demonstrates the attitude of Israel toward God at the time. She was weary of God and His ways. There was no delight in her heart for God. The thrill of knowing the King of kings had waned. The enjoyment of fellowship with her Creator had faded. Other things had captured her attention and drawn her away. The question, "how have I wearied you?" is one God could easily be asking us today. Have there not been times in our lives when we have lost the sense of joy in the Lord. This was the case for David after his sin with Bathsheba. Listen to his prayer in Psalm 51:12:

(12) Restore to me the joy of your salvation, and uphold me with a willing spirit. - Psalms 51:12 ESV

The psalmist's heart was grieved when the joy of his salvation seemed to dwindle after his sin. He cried out to God for its restoration. He understood that this lack of joy was not a healthy experience. Those who know the salvation of God were to experience "pleasures forevermore."

(11) You make known to me the path of life; in your presence there is fullness of joy; at your right hand are pleasures forevermore. - Psalms 16:11 ESV

It is for this reason that the psalmist cried out in Psalm 85:

(6) Will you not revive us again, that your people may rejoice in you? - Psalms 85:6 ESV

The psalmist understood how easy it is for the human heart to be distracted from the beauty and delight of God. He cried out for a revival of rejoicing in the Lord. Has God become wearisome to you? How we need to experience this revival in our hearts. Israel had fallen into this weariness. Her eyes had been blinded to the beauty of her God. Her heart had become so hard with sin that she no longer experienced joy in her Creator and Saviour.

How striking it is that God would take up this case against His people. It grieved God's heart deeply, however, that His people were not rejoicing in Him. Do you realize that it is the heart of God that we delight in Him? Do you know that it is His purpose that we experience great joy in Him and His work in us? Could it be that the charge God brings against Israel could easily have been brought against us today? How much He has done for us, and how deeply He cares. May our hearts once again leap for joy in knowing and experiencing Him.

What Does God Require?

For Prayer:

Father, as we consider these verses in Micah 6, we understand that You called Your people to account for their lack of delight and confidence in You. We recognize that Your ways are not the same as our ways. We confess that we do not always understand Your purpose. Teach us, however, to trust what You are doing. Restore to us the joy of our salvation. Forgive us for allowing lesser things to distract us from Your beauty. Reveal Yourself to us in such a way that it removes all temptation to question Your ways. Give us a heart that once again longs for You and Your presence.

Chapter 2 - With What Shall I Come Before the Lord?

6 "With what shall I come before the LORD, and bow myself before God on high? - Mi 6:6a, ESV

Micah 6:1-5 details the case between God and His people. In these verses, God demonstrated that He had faithfully cared for His people from their bondage in Egypt until they arrived in the Promised Land. He proved beyond a shadow of a doubt that He had been faithful to His covenantal agreement with His people. Israel was left without defence and found guilty of abandoning her legally binding covenant with God.

This guilty verdict humbled the children of Israel, and they were forced to reconsider their obligation to their Creator. As we come to verse 6, God's people ask an important question:

6 "With what shall I come before the LORD, and bow myself before God on high? – Micah 6:6a ESV

There are several details we need to see in this section of verse 6.

Notice first that Israel recognizes her guilt. In Micah 6:1-5, God had asked her what He had done to them and how He had wearied them. This question shows that Israel had accused God of wrongdoing. She had also found Him and His ways wearisome. As a result, she abandoned Him to serve other gods. This is very clear from the words of God in Micah 5:12-14:

(12) and I will cut off sorceries from your hand, and you shall have no more tellers of fortunes; (13) and I will cut off your carved images and your pillars from among you, and you shall bow down no more to the work of your hands; (14) and I will root out your Asherah images from among you and destroy your cities. - Micah 5:11-14 ESV

These words from God show us that Israel had become involved in sorcery, fortune-telling and bowing down to carved images and pillars. They had been unfaithful to God and worshipped other gods. The trial of Micah 6:1-5 declared her guilty, and she was forced to accept her sinful ways. Now in the opening section of Micah 6:6, she asks:

6 "With what shall I come before the LORD, and bow myself before God on high? – Micah 6:6 ESV

This statement is a recognition of guilt and an attempt to correct her ways.

Second, notice the expectation of the people of God. They anticipated that they could come before the Lord. This is a bold statement. They had been unfaithful to Him and falsely declared that He had wronged them. They were guilty of unfaithfulness. Why should God allow them to approach? Why should He open His heart to them after what they had done to Him and what they had said about Him? Israel, however, expected that her God would show mercy upon her and forgive her sin.

Third, the words *"with what shall I come before the Lord, and bow myself before God on high?"* show us that Israel wanted to approach her God and bow before Him. This bowing was a sign of respect and humility. It was a declaration of her willingness to submit to God as her one true God. By declaring Him to be the "God on high," she recognized Him to be God over all gods.

Notice, however, that she does not want to come empty-handed to God. She felt the need to bring something with her. "With what shall I come before the Lord?" she asked. Remember here that Micah 6 speaks about the chosen people of God. He had chosen them from all other people on the earth. They belonged to Him and were bound to Him by an eternal covenant. They had good reason to ask, "with what shall I come before the Lord and bow myself before God on high?" They were the favoured ones to whom God had revealed His presence and pardon. They owed Him much.

As the children of God in Micah's day, if you know the Lord Jesus as your Lord and Saviour, consider the immense privilege you have. The Creator God has chosen to reveal Himself to you. He has pardoned you and prepares a place in heaven for you to live forever with Him. The Spirit of God dwells in you, giving you spiritual life, understanding and empowerment. He has given you ears to hear His voice (Matthew 11:15, John 10:27). The Holy Spirit has been transforming you and producing His fruit in you (Galatians 5:22).

Shall we who have received such gifts stand before Him with nothing to show for a life lived under His pardon? This section of Micah 6:6 speaks to all who know the forgiveness and life of God in them. As you consider standing before the Lord God when this life of earth is over, with what shall you come before Him? What will you place at His feet as an offering of praise and thanksgiving?

Understand that it was not because Israel deserved His favour that God chose to love her. He reminds her of this in Deuteronomy 7 when He says:

(6) "For you are a people holy to the LORD your God. The LORD your God has chosen you to be a people for his treasured possession, out of all the peoples who are on the face of the earth. (7) It was not because you were more in number than any other people that the LORD set his love on you and chose you, for you were the fewest of all peoples, (8) but it is because the LORD loves you and is keeping the oath that he swore to your fathers, that the LORD has brought you out with a mighty hand and redeemed you from the house of slavery, from the hand of Pharaoh king of Egypt. - Deuteronomy 7:6-8 ESV

What does a newly born infant have to offer the mother who just gave birth? That helpless child can give nothing to the mother in return. The infant is totally dependant on her for everything. This is how it is for all who are born into the family of God. We enter like children with nothing. While we cannot pay for our salvation, we must live a life filled with gratitude and praise for this new birth. Listen to the words of Paul in Romans 14:

(12) So then each of us will give an account of himself to God. - Romans 14:12 ESV

Knowing this, each of us must ask the question: *"With what shall I come before the Lord and bow myself before God on high?"* Consider the forgiveness of God and His provision and protection from Egypt to Gilgal (from your release from bondage until you arrive in the Promised Land). Reflect on His promise of joy forever in His presence. Take a moment to think about the cost of this forgiveness and eternal life. Shall we stand empty-handed before Him who has done so much for us? Do you not find yourself asking the same question as the people of Micah's day? "With what shall I come before the LORD and bow myself before God on high?" What could I possibly offer the God from whom all blessings flow? What would a holy and righteous God want from me? While Micah will go on to provide an answer to this question, one thing is sure. This gracious God deserves much more than empty hands and a wasted life. If I am to stand before Him, I must find an answer to this question.

For Prayer:

Father, we confess that we have been like your people in Micah 6. We are guilty before you. We have grumbled and complained about Your purpose for our lives. We have failed to understand the immense privilege we have to be Your children. We have not always been grateful for your grace. Thank you, Father, that while we have not been the children You called us to be, You forgive us and continue to draw us to Yourself. Lord, would you give us a deeper appreciation for what You have done and are continuing to do in us. Teach us to make our lives count for You. We know that we brought nothing into our salvation but may we, by Your grace, produce wonderful fruit for your glory. Thank you, Holy Spirit, that You enable us and instruct us in how we should walk. Thank you that in You and by Your enabling, we can produce much fruit. As we continue in this study, teach us the kind of fruit you want from us.

Chapter 3 - Burnt Offerings and One-Year-Old Calves

6 Shall I come before him with burnt offerings, with calves a year old? - Micah 6:6

In the case between God and His people, Israel was found guilty of unfaithfulness. They had failed in their obligations toward their Creator. Unsure of where to go from here, the people of Micah's day asked: "With what shall I come before the LORD and bow myself before God on high?" (Micah 6:1a). Israel expressed her uncertainty about what God required and how she was to live before Him in asking this question.

Recognize that in Micah 6:1-5, God demonstrated how much He had cared for her. He rescued her from Egypt and brought her through the wilderness. He protected Israel from the curse of Balaam and settled her in the Promised Land. Israel was so blinded by selfishness and lust that she failed to appreciate what her Creator had done.

As her eyes were opened to her guilt, she came to realize her indebtedness to the Lord. As He confronted her sin, she began to understand that she had an obligation toward Him. She had been called to be a light to the nations. She had been chosen to be a servant of the Almighty. At that moment, her focus was taken off herself and lifted to a higher purpose.

As she reflected on her future and what her response toward God ought to be, Israel asked for clarification through a series of questions. The first of those questions comes in the second part of verse 6:

6 Shall I come before him with burnt offerings, with calves a year old? - Micah 6:6

As Israel sought to understand what God required, her mind went back to the Law of Moses and the sacrifices and offerings it demanded. Two types of offerings are mentioned here –burnt offerings and sacrifices of one-year-old animals.

In Leviticus 1, Moses instructed his people to bring a bird or an offering from their livestock or flock as a burnt offering for sin. The Law of Moses required the sacrifice of a one-year-old animal on various occasions. A one-year-old calf and lamb were used in the ordination of the priests (Leviticus 9:3). A one-year-old lamb was necessary for purification from childbirth (Leviticus 12:6) or leprosy (Leviticus 14:10). The Israelites sacrificed a one-year-old lamb to give thanks for the first fruits of the harvest (Leviticus 23:12) and in the Passover celebration (Exodus 12:5).

The question we must ask this: Were these sacrifices first and foremost what God expected of Israel? Would God be satisfied if she observed all the religious celebrations found in the Law of Moses?

Let's put this in a modern-day context. What does God expect of us today? Would He be satisfied if we made going to church each Sunday a greater priority? Would He be pleased if we committed to reading the Bible from cover to cover every year? Would we be fulfilling our obligation to Him if we made it our commitment to witness to someone each day? Should I be fasting and praying more? Should I be giving more of my time and resources? The list could go on and on. Each of these activities is important and plays a role in the Christian life. The question, however, is whether, by doing all these things, we have fulfilled our obligation to God and pleased Him.

One day the Pharisees and Scribes came to Jesus and asked Him why His disciples did not follow the tradition of washing their hands before eating. Jesus responded by quoting from Isaiah the prophet:

(8) "'This people honors me with their lips, but their heart is far from me; (9) in vain do they worship me, teaching as doctrines the commandments of men.'" - Matthew 15:8-9 ESV

Jesus told the religious leaders that day that it was quite possible to go through the motions but have a heart that was not right with God. Jesus agreed with Isaiah when he said that this type of worship was in vain. Religious activities, in and of themselves, were not what God required.

The Pharisees and scribes were the most religious people in Jerusalem. They faithfully tithed, prayed and fasted. They kept themselves from any impurity and refused to associate with sinners. Notice, however, what the Lord Jesus had to say about them in Matthew 23:

(27) "Woe to you, scribes and Pharisees, hypocrites! For you are like whitewashed tombs, which outwardly appear beautiful, but within are full of dead people's bones and all uncleanness. (28) So you also outwardly appear righteous to others, but within you are full of hypocrisy and lawlessness. - Matthew 23:27-28 ESV

Jesus had harsher words to speak to these religious Pharisees and scribes than any other group. He told those who listened to Him one day that they would never see the kingdom of heaven unless their righteousness surpassed that of the Pharisees:

(20) For I tell you, unless your righteousness exceeds that of the scribes and Pharisees, you will never enter the kingdom of heaven. - Matthew 5:20 ESV

For the Pharisee, God required strict adherence to religious duty. Jesus informed them, however, that their religion was vain and that all their efforts would never please the Father enough to let them into heaven.

Listen to the words of the apostle Paul to the Colossians:

(20) If with Christ you died to the elemental spirits of the world, why, as if you were still alive in the world, do you submit to regulations— (21) "Do not handle, Do not taste, Do not touch" (22) (referring to things that all perish as they are used)—according to human precepts and teachings? (23) These have indeed an appearance of wisdom in promoting self-made religion and asceticism and severity to the body, but they are of no value in stopping the indulgence of the flesh. - Colossians 2:20-23 ESV

Paul speaks in Colossians 2 to a people whose faith consisted of a series of rules and regulations – "Do not handle, Do not taste, Do not touch." He told the Colossians that these rules had "an appearance of wisdom" but promoted a "self-made religion" that had no value in stopping the "indulgence of the flesh." In other words, this legalistic religion had no power to change human nature. Not touching something doesn't mean you don't want to touch it.

Speaking about his brothers and sisters in the Jewish faith, the apostle Paul said:

(1) Brothers, my heart's desire and prayer to God for them is that they may be saved. (2) For I bear them witness that they have a zeal for God, but not according to knowledge. (3) For, being ignorant of the righteousness of God, and seeking to establish their own, they did not submit to God's righteousness. - Romans 10:1-3 ESV

The Jews, Paul speaks about here, sought to establish their own righteousness. In other words, they sought to obtain a right standing with God through their religious efforts. This is often the problem with religion. It promotes human effort to gain God's favour and blessing.

Even as true believers, we can fall into this trap. It is easy to believe that if we pray more, God will be more pleased with us. If we read our Bible more, He will want to be closer to us. If we live a certain lifestyle, we will be more spiritual. All of these things draw attention away from God and the inner work of the Spirit to our efforts. While I am certainly not diminishing the importance of these spiritual exercises, God will not love me more if I pray more, nor will he love me less if I serve Him less. The father's love for the prodigal son in Luke 15 was as great as his love for the son who stayed home. We have all met religious people who would never miss a Sunday church service but whose lives do not demonstrate the inner work of God's Spirit, transforming them into the image of Christ.

The question, "Shall I come before him with burnt offerings, with calves a year old?" is one we all need to consider. Is the observation of religious traditions what God primarily requires? Or is there something more? As important as our observation of the traditions and commandments is, is it not possible for us to follow all of these religiously and still not be in a right relationship with God?

What Does God Require?

As you examine your walk with God today, what is it all about? How would you define your relationship with Him? Is it all about church, religious rituals and obligations? Is this all that God requires? Would you describe your relationship with your husband or wife in the same way? Does your relationship with your children consist only of duties, obligations, and rules? While these things may be important, it seems that a relationship with God is much more than external obligations and responsibilities. We can do all this and still fall short of what God requires.

For Prayer:

Thank you, Lord Jesus, for coming to earth and laying down your life on the cross for me. I recognize that You did not die so that we could go to church and follow a set of religious duties. While these things are important, You had something much greater in mind. Thank you that Your death sets me free from the penalty of sin and a futile human effort to please you by my religious activities. What You did on the cross gives me a right standing with God. I don't have to add anything more to what You have done to be completely accepted and forgiven by the Father. No religious effort on my part can make me any more accepted and forgiven. You have done all that is necessary. Teach me now to serve and worship from a heart that is completely loved and pardoned. May my service flow from a grateful heart. May my worship be the expression of a heart transformed by the inner work of the Spirit of God who dwells within.

Chapter 4 - Rivers of Oil

7 Will the LORD be pleased with thousands of rams, with ten thousands of rivers of oil? - Micah 6:7 ESV

God's people have been trying to understand what God required of them. In verse 6, they asked about offering Him burnt offerings and sacrifices of one-year-old calves. We move now to their second suggestion – "thousands of rams, with ten thousands of rivers of oil" (Micah 6:7a ESV).

Both of these articles were used to worship God at this time. Rams were used for sacrifices (Exodus 29:15-16; Leviticus 5:15), and oil was poured on offerings:

1 "When anyone brings a grain offering as an offering to the LORD, his offering shall be of fine flour. He shall pour oil on it and put frankincense on it – Leviticus 2:1 ESV

While Israel has already asked about bringing burnt offerings and sacrifices to the Lord in verse 6, her question here is different. Notice the number of rams and the quantity of oil in verse 7. Israel speaks in verse 7 about thousands of rams and ten thousands of rivers of oil. The idea here is that one burnt offering and a small quantity of oil might not be sufficient. If they increased the number of offerings, would this please God more?

Maybe you take twenty minutes every day to read a portion of Scripture and pray. Would God be more pleased with you if you spent thirty minutes instead? Would He pour out more blessings if you chose to go to another church meeting every week? Would it delight His heart more if you put extra money in the offering? Can we buy His favour with more money and more time?

There is no question that the Lord God deserves everything we have. Of course, there is more we can do for the kingdom of God. However, we must ask whether the quantity of money we give and the number of sacrifices we make are God's primary focus.

One day Jesus was in the temple and sat down opposite the treasury. He sat there watching people putting money into the offering box. Listen to the account of this event as recorded by Mark:

> *(41) And he sat down opposite the treasury and watched the people putting money into the offering box. Many rich people put in large sums. (42) And a poor widow came and put in two small copper coins, which make a penny. (43) And he called his disciples to him and said to them, "Truly, I say to you, this poor widow has put in more than all those who are contributing to the offering box. (44) For they all contributed out of their abundance, but she out of her poverty has put in everything she had, all she had to live on." - Mark 12:41-44 ESV*

The rich contributed money out of their abundance, but the poor widow only gave two small coins equaling a penny. Jesus, however, was more impressed with this small gift than the abundance the rich people gave. For Jesus, this poor widow gave more because she willingly surrendered all she had left. One ram given with a right heart is of more value to God than ten thousand. How much we give is not what is important to God.

In the list of God's priorities, where does money or animal sacrifices fall? Consider the words of Samuel to Saul in 1 Samuel 15:

22 And Samuel said, "Has the LORD as great delight in burnt offerings and sacrifices, as in obeying the voice of the LORD? Behold, to obey is better than sacrifice, and to listen than the fat of rams. – 1 Samuel 15:22 ESV

Notice the words of Samuel here: "Has the LORD as great delight in burnt offerings and sacrifices, as in obeying?" In the mind of God, obedience is better than all the money or sacrifices we can bring Him.

Consider also the words of the Lord in Psalm 50:

9 I will not accept a bull from your house or goats from your folds. 10 For every beast of the forest is mine, the cattle on a thousand hills. 11 I know all the birds of the hills, and all that moves in the field is mine. 12 "If I were hungry, I would not tell you, for the world and its fullness are mine. - Psalms 50:9-12 ESV

God reminds us in Psalm 50 that the cattle on a thousand hills already belong to Him. The ten thousand rams we so proudly offer to God already belong to Him. If He wanted those rivers of oil, could He not take them whenever He wanted? Can we bring Him anything that is not already His?

Listen to the prophet Isaiah:

15 Behold, the nations are like a drop from a bucket, and are accounted as the dust on the scales; behold, he takes up the coastlands like fine dust. 16 Lebanon would not suffice for fuel, nor are its beasts enough for a burnt offering. 17 All the nations are as nothing before him, they are

*accounted by him as less than nothing and emptiness. 18
To whom then will you liken God, or what likeness compare
with him? - Isaiah 40:15-18 ESV*

When we understand who God is, would ten thousand rams and thousands of rivers of oil be a worthy gift? Isaiah tells us that all the nations of the earth with their combined wealth are but dust on a scale to Him. The entire forest of Lebanon would not provide enough wood for the sacrifices He deserved. There are not enough animals in the world to bring a worthy gift. If it belonged to us, everything we could offer would be an insult to the majesty and worth of this great and mighty God.

Listen to the response of God to His people in Amos 5:

21 "I hate, I despise your feasts, and I take no delight in your solemn assemblies. 22 Even though you offer me your burnt offerings and grain offerings, I will not accept them; and the peace offerings of your fattened animals, I will not look upon them. 23 Take away from me the noise of your songs; to the melody of your harps I will not listen. - Amos 5:21-23 ESV

It is only the mercy of God that accepts our worship and sacrifice. We are a sinful people. Every effort we make is tainted in one way or another by our sinful flesh. Who among us has not felt the desire for recognition in our service of the Lord? Who among us has not felt jealous of the blessings and success of other servants? Our sinful nature remains in us. What keeps God from rejecting our offerings? It is only because He is a God of grace that we can even approach Him.

The question Israel asks is this:

Rivers of Oil

7 Will the LORD be pleased with thousands of rams, with ten thousands of rivers of oil? - Micah 6:7 ESV

Is the priority of the Lord to receive large gifts and sacrifices from us? What use does God have for ten thousand dead rams sacrificed on an altar because His people sinned against Him? If the whole world belongs to Him, what can we offer that does not already belong to Him? While God graciously receives what we offer, this obviously is not primarily what He requires of us.

For Prayer:

Father God, we recognize You as the Creator and Owner of all things. We can offer nothing that is not already Yours. Everything we have is a gift from You. Help us never to hold so tightly to anything You give that we cannot surrender it to You should You require.

Forgive us for thinking that we could ever buy your favour with our offerings or sacrifices. Your love for us and devotion to us do not depend on how much we give to You. You love the rich as you love the poor. You love those confined to their sickbed as you love those sacrificing their lives on the mission fields of this world. Your love and favour are not bought and sold like fruit in a market.

We confess that there is no gift a mortal human being could offer that would be worthy of Your name. Our best is stained with sin and imperfect. We praise You, however, that You love us despite our imperfections and unworthiness. Thank you for the grace that reaches out and delights in those who cannot pay You back for Your generosity.

Chapter 5 - The Fruit of My Body

7 Shall I give my firstborn for my transgression, the fruit of my body for the sin of my soul?"- Micah 6:7b

Israel has been trying to understand what God required of her. In Micah 6:6,7, she asked Him about religious duty through burnt offerings and sacrifices. Uncertain that this was the answer, she suggested that maybe she could offer extravagant gifts of thousands of rams and rivers of oil. Considering that this might fall short, she makes her final offer, which was most precious to her –her firstborn child. If Israel's first two suggestions speak about religious duty and extravagant gifts, this last proposal relates to costly sacrifice.

Notice in verse 7 that Israel's concern is about her "transgression" and the "sin of her soul." As a nation, she had been unfaithful to God. She intended to make things right but was uncertain about how to do this. The proposal to offer her firstborn child suggests that she wonders if inflicting her soul with deep anguish might be what God required.

The hermit monk Anthony who lived from 251-356, gave away everything and went to live in the desert of Egypt. Simon the Stylite (390-459) chose to construct a small platform upon which to live. That platform was raised until it was estimated to be about 60 feet in the air. He lived on that platform for almost forty years. As part of Good Friday celebrations in the Philippines today, men and women choose to be nailed to a cross to reflect their devotion to God and penitence for their sin. Are these the kind of things God expects of us?

Living the Christian life will not be easy. Men and women around the world have suffered and died in the name of Christ. Jesus tells us that as the end approaches, there will be an increase in persecution:

(12) But before all this they will lay their hands on you and persecute you, delivering you up to the synagogues and prisons, and you will be brought before kings and governors for my name's sake. - Luke 21:12 ESV

Listen to what the apostle Paul told Timothy in 2 Timothy 3:12:

(12) Indeed, all who desire to live a godly life in Christ Jesus will be persecuted - 2 Timothy 3:12 ESV

There is no question that there will be great sacrifices and hardship for anyone serious about serving the Lord Jesus in this world. It is also clear that believers must be willing to endure these sufferings rather than deny their Lord.

(13) And you will be hated by all for my name's sake. But the one who endures to the end will be saved - Mark 13:13 ESV

As we stand before Him on that last day, will God be looking for how much we sacrificed and suffered for His name? Will this be the criteria upon which He judges us and our worthiness to enter His kingdom? Will our suffering and sacrifice here on earth bring us forgiveness and right standing with God?

The Only Sacrifice that Matters

While suffering and sacrifice are inevitable in a sinful world, none of this suffering can take away our guilt. Remember that Israel suggested offering her firstborn for the sin of her soul. The writer to the Hebrews tells us, however, that the blood of bulls and goats could not take away sin:

4 For it is impossible for the blood of bulls and goats to take away sins. - Hebrews 10:4 ESV

The apostles made it clear that there is salvation and forgiveness in no other name under heaven but the name of Jesus:

12 And there is salvation in no one else, for there is no other name under heaven given among men by which we must be saved." - Acts 4:12 ESV

There is only one person who can settle the dispute between God and man and bring total forgiveness and salvation:

5 For there is one God, and there is one mediator between God and men, the man Christ Jesus, - 1 Timothy 2:5 ESV

Paul told Romans that the sacrifice of Jesus Christ justified and saved them from the wrath of God. In other words, it paid off their debt and released them completely from the wrath and fiery judgement of God:

(8) but God shows his love for us in that while we were still sinners, Christ died for us. (9) Since, therefore, we have now been justified by his blood, much more shall we be saved by him from the wrath of God. - Romans 5:8-9 ESV

The blood of bulls and goats could not forgive us. There is no sacrifice we can make that will grant forgiveness and right standing with God. There is salvation and forgiveness in only one sacrifice – that of the perfect Lamb of God, Jesus Christ.

The Only Righteousness that Can be Credited to our Account

Consider also the words of Ezekiel 14:

> *13 "Son of man, when a land sins against me by acting faithlessly, and I stretch out my hand against it and break its supply of bread and send famine upon it, and cut off from it man and beast, 14 even if these three men, Noah, Daniel, and Job, were in it, they would deliver but their own lives by their righteousness, declares the Lord GOD. - Ezekiel 14:13-14 ESV*

In Ezekiel 14, the Lord told the prophet that when a land acted unfaithfully against Him and He punished its inhabitants, even if the great saints Noah, Daniel or Job were in their midst, it would not be spared God's wrath. The righteousness of these men would not be credited to them in their day of judgment.

Ezekiel takes this a step further in chapter 18:14-20. In this passage, the prophet describes a father who worships idols, commits adultery, robs and oppresses his neighbours. This father, however, has a son who rejected his father's ways and walked uprightly before the Lord. Ezekiel tells us that the father would die because of his iniquity, but his son would be spared:

> *(18) As for his father, because he practiced extortion, robbed his brother, and did what is not good among his people, behold, he shall die for his iniquity. (19) "Yet you say, 'Why should not the son suffer for the iniquity of the father?' When the son has done what is just and right, and*

*has been careful to observe all my statutes, he shall surely
live. -- Ezekiel 18:18-19 ESV*

The son would not die because of his father's evil. The father
alone would pay for his iniquity. The son did not bear his guilt.
Ezekiel concludes with this statement:

*(20) The soul who sins shall die. The son shall not suffer for
the iniquity of the father, nor the father suffer for the iniquity
of the son. The righteousness of the righteous shall be upon
himself, and the wickedness of the wicked shall be upon
himself. - Ezekiel 18:14-20 ESV*

The clear teaching of Ezekiel 18 is that I do not answer to God
for the sins of another person. The righteousness of another
human being cannot be credited to my account. An ungodly
child will not benefit from his father's godliness, nor will an
ungodly father be credited with his son's righteousness. Each
person will answer for their own life.

There is one exception to this rule. That exception once again
is found in the Lord Jesus. Listen to the prayer of the apostle
Paul for the Philippians:

*(9) And it is my prayer that your love may abound more and
more, with knowledge and all discernment, (10) so that you
may approve what is excellent, and so be pure and
blameless for the day of Christ, (11) filled with the fruit of
righteousness that comes through Jesus Christ, to the glory
and praise of God. - Philippians 1:9-11 ESV*

Notice that the apostle prayed that the Philippians would be
filled with the "fruit of righteousness that comes through Jesus
Christ." Paul spoke of this righteousness to the Corinthians
when he told them:

*(21) For our sake he made him to be sin who knew no sin,
so that in him we might become the righteousness of God. -
2 Corinthians 5:21 ESV*

Jesus Christ took on our sin and defeated it so that "we might become the righteousness of God." His work makes us right before God.

Finally, consider the words of Paul to the Romans when he said:

*(17) For if, because of one man's trespass, death reigned
through that one man, much more will those who receive the
abundance of grace and the free gift of righteousness reign
in life through the one man Jesus Christ. - Romans 5:17
ESV*

Paul speaks here of the "free gift of righteousness" that comes through Jesus Christ. All of these passages tell us that there is a righteousness that we obtain from the Lord Jesus. Righteousness is a right standing with God. No one but Jesus can give us this right standing with God. The righteousness that He gives as a gift is the only righteousness credited to our account.

Israel offered her firstborn. That firstborn, however, would never pay for her sin. There was no forgiveness in any other person but the Lord Jesus. Only He could restore the relationship between God and humankind. He alone was a perfect and acceptable sacrifice. While we may suffer in this life, our forgiveness and right standing with God is not based on how much we suffer or sacrifice for God but rather on what He suffered for us in the person of the Lord Jesus.

The Fruit of My Body

For Prayer:

Lord God, we recognize that each of us must answer for our sin. We also acknowledge that no personal sacrifice on our part could ever bring us forgiveness and right standing with you. I want to thank you for the grace that sent Your Son to this earth to die for me. I recognize that His sacrifice alone can bring me the pardon I so desperately need. He alone can give me right standing with God. Forgive me for feeling that if I suffer enough or give enough, I can gain your favour. Your favour is not bought and sold. It is freely offered through Jesus Christ to all who will accept it. Thank you that in Jesus Christ alone, I can find perfect acceptance and forgiveness. Thank you for revealing this truth to me and making it a reality through the work of Your Spirit in me.

Chapter 6 - He Has Told You

8 He has told you, O man, what is good; - Micah 6:8 ESV

The people of God have been seeking to understand the requirements of God for their lives. To this point, they had questioned God about religious duty, extravagant gifts, and costly sacrifices. As we come to verse 8, the Lord answers Israel's questions about what He expects of them. Notice the opening phrase of Micah 6:8:

8 He has told you, O man, what is good – Micah 6:8 ESV

Notice that Micah speaks in the past tense – "He has told you." In other words, the people of God were asking questions about something God had already revealed to them. He had already told them what He required. No further revelation was necessary. The answer to their questions was right before them.

The Hebrew word translated "told" in the English Standard Version of the Bible means to "make known," "to explain," or "to announce." Micah is telling His people that the God of Israel had already explained to them His requirements. The question we need to consider here is this: How had God made His purposes and requirements known to His people? The questions Israel has been asking in this passage indicate that they had missed this announcement. Let's consider how God spoke to His people in the Old Testament.

What Does God Require?

By His Creation

First, God spoke to His people in creation. Listen to the words of the psalmist in Psalm 19:

1 The heavens declare the glory of God, and the sky above proclaims his handiwork. 2 Day to day pours out speech, and night to night reveals knowledge. 3 There is no speech, nor are there words, whose voice is not heard. - Psalms 19:1-3 ESV

You can't read these verses without getting a sense of how loudly creation speaks. The heavens "declare the glory of God." The sky "proclaims His handiwork." Each new day "pours out speech." Every night "reveals knowledge." Creation speaks loudly about God and His purpose for this world. Who among us can look at a beautiful sunset and not see the artistry of the Creator? Who can look up into the vastness of the night sky and not see the immensity of our God? Can you watch a raging storm and not understand His fury and power? Do these things not humble us and bring us to our knees in gratitude and humility before the Creator?

Psalm 97 tells us something else about the voice of creation:

6 The heavens proclaim his righteousness, and all the peoples see his glory. 7 All worshipers of images are put to shame, who make their boast in worthless idols; worship him, all you gods! 8 Zion hears and is glad, and the daughters of Judah rejoice, because of your judgments, O LORD. 9 For you, O LORD, are most high over all the earth; you are exalted far above all gods. - Psalms 97:6-9 ESV

The psalmist tells us that the heavens proclaim the righteousness and glory of God, their Creator. When you consider that God created the heavens and the earth, you have no option but to be amazed at the majesty and wisdom of a God who could put this together. Now imagine that you lived in the days of Micah. You see people who take a tree and reshape it into an image. They then bow down to that image and worship it. What runs through your mind when you see this? Would it not horrify you that these individuals would bow down to a stick of wood and offer their worship and allegiance to it? Would you not question the wisdom of the idol worshipper and point them to the Creator God to whom we all owe our existence? Creation tells you that there is an infinitely wise God to whom all praise is due. Everything depends on Him. We owe our lives and worship to Him alone. God revealed what He required through creation.

By His Mighty Works

Not only did God speak through creation, but He revealed Himself even more personally to Israel through the works He did in their midst. Consider the words of Exodus 15:

11 "Who is like you, O LORD, among the gods? Who is like you, majestic in holiness, awesome in glorious deeds, doing wonders? 12 You stretched out your right hand; the earth swallowed them. 13 "You have led in your steadfast love the people whom you have redeemed; you have guided them by your strength to your holy abode. 14 The peoples have heard; they tremble; pangs have seized the inhabitants of Philistia. - Exodus 15:11-14 ESV

Exodus 15:11-14 shows us how God spoke to His people through His "glorious deeds." He did "wonders" among the children of Israel. He opened the earth and swallowed those who rebelled against His purposes (see Numbers 26:10). He also led His people with "steadfast love" through the wilderness to the Promised Land.

When God opened the earth to swallow those who rebelled against Him, He spoke loudly about what He required. When He protected and kept His people through the trials of the wilderness, He was communicating His purpose to them. Did God's people understand what He required when He opened up the sea for them to cross on dry ground? Did Joshua understand the purpose of God when He brought down the walls of Jericho after the priests blew their trumpets? Did King Darius understand what God required when He protected Daniel from the hungry lions? Throughout Israel's history, God revealed His purpose to His people by the works He did among them.

Through the Revelation of His Character

As the children of Israel reflected on the character of God revealed through creation, Law and mighty deeds, they couldn't help but understand His purpose. Consider the reflections of Jeremiah in this regard:

> 12   It is he who made the earth by his power, who established the world by his wisdom, and by his understanding stretched out the heavens. 13 When he utters his voice, there is a tumult of waters in the heavens, and he makes the mist rise from the ends of the earth. He makes lightning for the rain, and he brings forth the wind from his storehouses. - Jeremiah 10:12-13 ESV

Jeremiah considers here how the Lord made the earth by His great power. He saw the wisdom and understanding of God in the stretched out the heavens over the earth. He saw the power of God as He sent lightning and wind from the storehouses of heaven. Jeremiah understood God to be a God of wisdom, understanding and power. Understanding this, what would be His response when faced with the opposition of Israel to His preaching? Would He now question the wisdom of God who sent Him to His people? The more he understood and accepted the character of God, the more He could trust Him and step out into His purpose.

Exodus 19:18-21 tells us how God revealed His presence in the days of Moses:

18 Now Mount Sinai was wrapped in smoke because the LORD had descended on it in fire. The smoke of it went up like the smoke of a kiln, and the whole mountain trembled greatly. 19 And as the sound of the trumpet grew louder and louder, Moses spoke, and God answered him in thunder. 20 The LORD came down on Mount Sinai, to the top of the mountain. And the LORD called Moses to the top of the mountain, and Moses went up. 21 And the LORD said to Moses, "Go down and warn the people, lest they break through to the LORD to look and many of them perish.
- Exodus 19:18-21 ESV

God revealed Himself that day as a God of holiness. The fire and smoke caused the people to fear. The mountain trembled, and thunder roared as He spoke. Could you stand at the foot of that mountain and not take this God seriously? Could you witness such an incident without recognizing that this God deserved your respect and honour? God spoke to His people through the revelation of His character.

By His Dealings with Them

Let me extend this just a bit further by saying that God also spoke to His people through His interactions with them. The mighty works of God were evident in creation and history. But God also worked personally in the lives of individuals as well.

Consider the individual families in Israel as they wandered through the wilderness. Every day when they woke up, God provided manna to keep them alive and healthy. What did that tell them about God? What did God reveal about Himself to Achan when He required his life after he took forbidden articles from the city of Jericho? What was Mariam to think about God's requirements when He struck her with leprosy for disrespecting Moses? What did Abraham learn about God when He provided a ram to sacrifice in his son's place? The God of Israel spoke clearly to His people through His personal and individual dealings with them.

Through the Law and the prophet

Finally, and most clearly, God spoke to His people through the Law and the prophets:

> *30 Many years you bore with them and warned them by your Spirit through your prophets. Yet they would not give ear. Therefore you gave them into the hand of the peoples of the lands. - Nehemiah 9:30 ESV*

God spoke to His people by communicating specific messages to them through His prophets. A good part of the Old Testament is taken up with the words of these prophets. God also revealed His requirements to Israel through His commandments and laws:

8 And you shall again obey the voice of the LORD and keep all his commandments that I command you today. 9 The LORD your God will make you abundantly prosperous in all the work of your hand, in the fruit of your womb and in the fruit of your cattle and in the fruit of your ground. For the LORD will again take delight in prospering you, as he took delight in your fathers, 10 when you obey the voice of the LORD your God, to keep his commandments and his statutes that are written in this Book of the Law, when you turn to the LORD your God with all your heart and with all your soul. - Deuteronomy 30:8-10 ESV

The "Book of the Law" given through Moses showed God's people the kind of life He required of them. He promised that by observing that Law, they would prosper under His blessing. God felt so strongly that His people should understand this Law that He had it written down and preserved. The Law revealed God's requirements and purpose for His people. When Micah told the people of Israel that God had told them what is good, he reminded Israel of the many ways their Creator had been speaking to them.

Let's consider what Micah told the people of Israel in our modern context. Some time ago, I spoke to a pastor who was struggling with an issue in his church. He had been asking other pastors how they would deal with a similar situation in their church. I suggested a passage of Scripture that addressed this particularly, but the questions continued. I was left with the impression that he was looking for something more than what this passage of Scripture revealed.

Over the years, I have watched church after church searching for some programme or discipleship course that will transform their church into a dynamic and vibrant fellowship. We read book after book to find out how we can get closer to God. We attend one conference after another in the hope of finding some new revelation about deeper empowerment and intimacy with God. It seems that there are people constantly seeking some new insight that will unlock the secrets of the Christian life. I have to admire this devotion to seek after God. My concern, however, is not that we want to grow but where we are searching for answers.

The words, "he has told you, O man, what is good," speak to us today. All too many people search for this good outside of what God has already revealed. Instead of seeking a new revelation that will unlock the secrets of the Christian life, we need to listen to the old revelations of God from the beginning of time. The secret is not new. God has already made it plain. Do you want to know what God requires, then look to what He has already revealed? Do you want to know how your church can grow and impact this world, then you need to see what He teaches in the written revelation He has already given? It is not some new revelation we need but obedience to the revelation He has already given. As we seek Him, may God open our eyes and ears to the many ways He has already revealed Himself to us.

For Prayer:

Lord God, forgive us for our spiritual blindness. Open our deafened ears to hear what You are revealing to us. Help us see what You are revealing to us about Yourself and Your purpose for our lives. Thank you for your inspired and authoritative Word. Thank you for Your Spirit who has been given to reveal Your purpose. Open our eyes to see Your presence in the many things that take place each day. We are grateful for the many ways you have worked in our lives and

He Has Told You

what those ways have taught us about You. Draw near to us as we learn to walk in Your purpose.

Chapter 7 - Do Justice

8 and what does the LORD require of you but to do justice -
Micah 6:8 ESV

We come now to Micah's answer to what God required of His people. In verse eight, Micah speaks about three requirements of God. The first of these is to do justice.

When we hear the word "justice," we usually think of a criminal standing before a judge to receive punishment for a crime. Notice, however, that Micah speaks here about doing justice. Justice, according to Micah, is a way of life. Probably the best way to understand this is to examine how other Old Testament writers define this concept.

Micah is not the only Old Testament writer to teach that justice is something we do. Listen to the words of God concerning Abraham:

19 For I have chosen him, that he may command his children and his household after him to keep the way of the LORD by doing righteousness and justice, so that the LORD may bring to Abraham what he has promised him." -
Genesis 18:19 ESV

God chose Abraham for a purpose. According to Genesis 18:19, that purpose was to teach his children to do righteousness and justice. God desired that Abraham's descendants learn to live a life of righteousness and justice.

The psalmist says something very similar when he tells us that God does justice to the fatherless and oppressed:

17 O LORD, you hear the desire of the afflicted; you will strengthen their heart; you will incline your ear 18 to do justice to the fatherless and the oppressed, so that man who is of the earth may strike terror no more. - Psalms 10:17-18 ESV

The Psalmist tells us that God inclines His ear to the orphan and the oppressed. He sees their suffering and will "do justice" so their oppressors will no longer strike terror in their hearts. The sense here is that God would stop the oppression of those suffering unjustly at the hands of greedy and cruel men. To do justice, in this sense, is to take up the cause of the needy and bring an end to their suffering and pain.

Deuteronomy 10 takes this a step further when it says:

17 For the LORD your God is God of gods and Lord of lords, the great, the mighty, and the awesome God, who is not partial and takes no bribe. 18 He executes justice for the fatherless and the widow, and loves the sojourner, giving him food and clothing. 19 Love the sojourner, therefore, for you were sojourners in the land of Egypt. - Deuteronomy 10:17-19 ESV

Notice in Deuteronomy 10 that God executes justice for the fatherless, widow, and foreigner. Of interest here is how God does this. First, by not being partial or taking bribes. God treats the helpless as He treats the wealthy and prosperous. He does not judge the value of an individual by what they have or do not have. Nor will he give special favours to the rich over the poor. Second, by giving them food and clothing. According to Deuteronomy 10, justice is more than an attitude; it is also an action. To do justice is to provide clothing and food to those in need. It is to ease their suffering.

To do justice, according to Deuteronomy 24, is to refrain from putting another person under undue hardship:

17 "You shall not pervert the justice due to the sojourner or to the fatherless, or take a widow's garment in pledge, - Deuteronomy 24:17 ESV

In Bible times, when an individual owed money, they gave something to their creditor to guarantee that they would pay what they owed. In Deuteronomy 24, we have the case of a poor widow owing money to a creditor. If this creditor took her only garment in pledge, she would have nothing to keep warm at night. In this case, the just thing to do was not to take this pledge because it would put this widow under undue hardship. True justice requires consideration of another person's needs. It will suffer loss rather than cause unnecessary trouble for a brother or sister.

Isaiah 1 teaches us that doing justice will sometimes require political or legal action.

17 learn to do good; seek justice, correct oppression; bring justice to the fatherless, plead the widow's cause. - Isaiah 1:17 ESV

According to Isaiah, believers were to learn how to correct oppression in their society. They were to stand up for the most vulnerable and plead their cause. The just person has a heart for those who are suffering. They will do all they can to care for the needy and oppressed. They will seek to bring change to their society so that no one suffers from a lack of resources.

Jeremiah 7:5-7 explains quite clearly what it means to do justice:

What Does God Require?

5 "For if you truly amend your ways and your deeds, if you truly execute justice one with another, 6 if you do not oppress the sojourner, the fatherless, or the widow, or shed innocent blood in this place, and if you do not go after other gods to your own harm, 7 then I will let you dwell in this place, in the land that I gave of old to your fathers forever. - Jeremiah 7:5-7 ESV

Jeremiah calls his people to "execute justice one with another." In verse six, he defines this justice as not oppressing the sojourner, fatherless or widow, shedding innocent blood or going after other gods to their harm.

Jeremiah teaches that justice is not just refraining from oppressing the needy; it also involves delivering them from the hand of their oppressors.

3 Thus says the LORD: Do justice and righteousness and deliver from the hand of the oppressor him who has been robbed. And do no wrong or violence to the resident alien, the fatherless, and the widow, nor shed innocent blood in this place. - Jeremiah 22:3 ESV

From these Old Testament verses, we can see that justice is much more than standing before a judge to receive a sentence. Biblical justice relates to doing what is right for those who are oppressed and needy. It demands a sacrifice of time and resources. Doing justice demands taking up the cause of the widow, the orphan, the elderly, or the sick.

This principle of justice continues in the New Testament. Jesus demonstrated this by healing the sick and ministering to those who were the outcasts of society. This earned him the name "a friend of tax collectors and sinners."

(34) The Son of Man has come eating and drinking, and you say, 'Look at him! A glutton and a drunkard, a friend of tax collectors and sinners!' - Luke 7:34 ESV

As the apostles began their ministry, they not only preached the gospel but healed the sick. Their concern was for the whole person, body, soul and spirit.

The early church made doing justice such a priority that they willingly sold their possessions so that the proceeds could be distributed to the needy among them:

(43) And awe came upon every soul, and many wonders and signs were being done through the apostles. (44) And all who believed were together and had all things in common. (45) And they were selling their possessions and belongings and distributing the proceeds to all, as any had need. - Acts 2:43-45 ESV

This vision resulted in a daily distribution of food and provisions to widows:

(1) Now in these days when the disciples were increasing in number, a complaint by the Hellenists arose against the Hebrews because their widows were being neglected in the daily distribution. - Acts 6:1 ESV

In his first letter to Timothy, Paul gave Timothy guidelines on carrying out a regular ministry to the widows in his church (see 1 Timothy 5).

James defines pure religion in the following terms:

(27) Religion that is pure and undefiled before God the Father is this: to visit orphans and widows in their affliction, and to keep oneself unstained from the world. - James 1:27 ESV

For the apostle James, a genuine faith was on that practiced justice.

There can be no doubt that God requires justice. It is His nature to care for the outcast and needy. He reached out to us in our need and cared for us. He expects us to do no less. If we want to do justice as a church, we cannot be concerned only for ourselves. We must be a people who value justice by opening our eyes and hands to the weary and mistreated around us.

We began by stating that God chose Abraham so that "*he may command his children and his household after him to keep the way of the LORD by doing righteousness and justice*" *(Genesis 18:19)*. It was the purpose of God that His people be a people of justice, caring for and fighting for those in need. He has placed us on this earth to make a difference in the lives of those around us. By doing justice, we fulfill the mandate of God.

Micah tells us that God requires that we do justice. The word "require" is important. It tells us that if we fail in this matter of justice, we have failed in our responsibility toward God. God has given us the responsibility to care for our brother and sister. He has charged us with the responsibility to minister to the poor and needy among us. We must ask God to open our eyes to see the pain in our midst. If we are to do justice as He requires, we will need to plead with Him to give us a willing and sacrificial heart to care for those He places before us.

For Prayer:

Lord God, thank you for showing us what it means to do justice. We confess that we have often been selfish and thought only of ourselves. We also acknowledge that instead of ministering to the outcasts in our society, we have run from them. We pray that you would give us a heart for justice. Open our eyes and hearts to the needy among us. We recognize that You have called us not just to preach the gospel in words but also to demonstrate the justice of God through our actions. Forgive our failures and give us courage and wisdom to know how you would have us do justice in our circle of influence.

Chapter 8 - Loving Kindness

8 and to love kindness, - Micah 6:8 ESV

Micah has been explaining what God requires from His people. He reminded them first in Micah 6:8 that God wanted them to "do justice." The second requirement of God, according to Micah, is kindness. The Hebrew word used here is " חֶסֶד *ḥeseḏ.*" It can be translated by "kindness, mercy, goodness, faithfulness, or love." The word appears twenty-six times in Psalm 136 and is translated as "steadfast love" in the English Standard Version. A quick look at this psalm helps us better understand what Micah means by kindness.

Psalm 136 is a psalm of praise to the Lord for His "steadfast love" (ESV), or mercy (KJV). In the first nine verses, the psalmist describes how the Lord did wonders (verse 4), made the heavens (verse 5), spread out the earth (verse 6), and created the great lights (verses 7-9). All of this is a gift from our Creator for us to enjoy. It is a powerful demonstration of His extravagant generosity and kindness.

The psalmist goes on in the remainder of the psalm to describe how God struck down the firstborn of Egypt when Israel was held in captivity (verse 10). He reminds his people of how God brought Israel out of their bondage (verses 11-12), divided the sea and led Israel through the wilderness (verses 13-16). God protected His people in that wilderness, provided them with daily food (verse 25) and gave them their own land (verses 17-25). Verse 23 sums up what the psalmist is communicating:

(23) It is he who remembered us in our low estate, for his steadfast love endures forever; - Psalms 136:23 ESV

The God of mercy and steadfast love reached out to His people to protect and provide for their every need. He kept them from their enemies and led them through every obstacle they encountered. This, according to the psalmist, was a wonderful example of God's kindness to a people of "low estate" or of little significance.

The kindness of God was offered to those who did not deserve or merit it. Listen to the words of the Lord to Israel in Deuteronomy 7:

7 It was not because you were more in number than any other people that the LORD set his love on you and chose you, for you were the fewest of all peoples, 8 but it is because the LORD loves you and is keeping the oath that he swore to your fathers, that the LORD has brought you out with a mighty hand and redeemed you from the house of slavery, from the hand of Pharaoh king of Egypt. - Deuteronomy 7:7-8 ESV

In choosing Israel to be the object of His kindness, God chose a small and insignificant people. Those who were blessed by this love often proved to be unfaithful, but God's kindness endured.

The book of Hosea paints a very intimate picture of the relationship between God and His people. It does this by sharing the struggle of Hosea with his unfaithful wife. Listen to what God asked Hosea to do in Hosea 3:

1 And the LORD said to me, "Go again, love a woman who is loved by another man and is an adulteress, even as the

Loving Kindness

LORD loves the children of Israel, though they turn to other gods and love cakes of raisins."- Hosea 3:1 ESV

Hosea's wife, Gomer, was committing adultery. She allowed herself to be loved by another man. God told Hosea to take her back and love her as He loved Israel, who was also unfaithful. The kindness and steadfast love of God was stronger than the rebellion of His people. His kindness transcends rejection and unfaithfulness.

The mercy and kindness of God are seen in how He forgives sin committed against Him. David wrote Psalm 51 after committing adultery with Bathsheba and having her husband murdered to cover it up. Listen to His words:

(1) Have mercy on me, O God, according to your steadfast love; according to your abundant mercy blot out my transgressions. (2) Wash me thoroughly from my iniquity, and cleanse me from my sin! (3) For I know my transgressions, and my sin is ever before me. (4) Against you, you only, have I sinned and done what is evil in your sight, so that you may be justified in your words and blameless in your judgment. - Psalms 51:1-4 ESV

Here in this prayer of David, we see the king pleading with God for mercy because of His sin. David approached God because he knew Him to be a God of compassion and kindness, extending forgiveness to the undeserving. God's heart is revealed in His willingness to forgive those who offended Him.

In Matthew 18, Jesus told the story of a king who wanted to settle his accounts with his servants. A man was brought before him, who owed him ten thousand talents. The servant confessed that he could not pay, so the king ordered that he and his family be sold into slavery until they had worked off their debt. When he pleaded with the king for mercy, he generously forgave him and released him from his debt.

Jesus told His listeners that when that forgiven servant left the king's presence, he found a fellow servant who owed him just one hundred denarii. He seized his fellow servant and demanded payment of what he owed. When this servant pleaded with him for time, the servant who had been forgiven his great debt refused to give him time and cast him into prison until he could pay what he owed. When news of this reached the king's ears, he summoned the man he had forgiven and said:

> 33   And should not you have had mercy on your fellow
> servant, as I had mercy on you?' – Matthew 18:33 ESV

Notice how the king told this servant that he should have had mercy on his fellow servant. That mercy was to be demonstrated in a willingness to suffer loss to ease the burden from his brother's shoulders.

While justice gives people what they deserve, mercy and kindness give them what they do not always deserve. Kindness reaches out in extravagant blessing to those who sometimes reject it. It forgives those who have offended and will willingly suffer personal loss to ease the burden of a brother or sister.

The apostle Paul sets up the Lord Jesus as an example of kindness and mercy when he writes:

> (3) Do nothing from selfish ambition or conceit, but in
> humility count others more significant than yourselves. (4)
> Let each of you look not only to his own interests, but also to
> the interests of others. (5) Have this mind among

yourselves, which is yours in Christ Jesus, (6) who, though he was in the form of God, did not count equality with God a thing to be grasped, (7) but emptied himself, by taking the form of a servant, being born in the likeness of men. (8) And being found in human form, he humbled himself by becoming obedient to the point of death, even death on a cross. - Philippians 2:3-8 ESV

The Lord Jesus lived a selfless life. He devoted Himself to ministering to others and sacrificed Himself to care for them in their need. He endured suffering and loss so that those who came to Him would be blessed. That merciful kindness resulted in the salvation and forgiveness of His people:

(4) But when the goodness and loving kindness of God our Savior appeared, (5) he saved us, not because of works done by us in righteousness, but according to his own mercy, by the washing of regeneration and renewal of the Holy Spirit, (6) whom he poured out on us richly through Jesus Christ our Savior, (7) so that being justified by his grace we might become heirs according to the hope of eternal life. - Titus 3:4-7 ESV

When Micah tells us that God requires kindness, He tells us that we who have received such riches and blessing from God must be willing to do the same for others. We who have been so wonderfully forgiven must extend this same forgiveness to our brothers and sisters. We who have experienced the salvation of God through the extravagant sacrifice of Jesus must also be willing to surrender our time and resources for the good of those He sends our way.

Notice something else in 6:8. The prophet tells us that we are to "love" kindness. There is a world of difference between loving kindness and being kind to be noticed. It is one thing to give with a grudging spirit and quite another to give with a heart full of love and willing surrender. God does not just require kindness here. He is asking for a love of kindness. The kind of person Micah speaks about will give generously from a heart that can't help but respond to the needs of a brother or sister. It is a heart that wants more than anything to forgive those who have offended them. It loves to bless an enemy. It is the heart of a person who will sacrifice everything with no motive apart from a passionate desire to minister to the needs of those around them.

A kind or merciful person loves to bless others by sacrificing themselves, their time or possessions. Kind people will suffer loss for an enemy. They will endure rejection but not hold this against those who reject them. They will forgive the greatest hurt and respond with blessing and compassion to those who have offended them.

God does not ask us to do anything here He has not already done for us. If anything, He is asking us to treat others as He has treated us. We are to show the world what God has done for us by our acts of kindness and mercy. We are to testify to His kindness by our actions toward others. They are to see a picture of God through our efforts and how we treat one another.

Listen to the words of the Lord Jesus in John 13:

(34) A new commandment I give to you, that you love one another: just as I have loved you, you also are to love one another. (35) By this all people will know that you are my disciples, if you have love for one another." - John 13:34-35 ESV

Jesus commanded His followers to love each other as He loved them. He told them that people would know they were

His disciples by how they loved each other. We can testify to the loving-kindness of the Saviour with our words, but unless we demonstrate this by our actions, who will believe our words?

For Prayer:

Lord God, we have often taken what You do for us for granted. We confess that Your kindness toward us has richly blessed us. Thank you for life, salvation and uncountable blessings. Forgive us for not sharing that kindness with others. Forgive us for turning our back on brother or sister who has offended us. Forgive us for our unwillingness to sacrifice our blessings to minister to a brother or sister in need. Teach us to forgive as you forgave us. Give us a heart that loves mercy and kindness. May it delight our soul to love others as You have loved us. Teach us to follow the example of Jesus, who left the glories of heaven to die for unworthy humans. May we testify to Your kindness by our actions and relationships with those around us. May people see who You are by how we respond to one another.

Chapter 9 - Walking Humbly with God

8 and to walk humbly with your God? - Micah 6:8 ESV

The final requirement of God in Micah 6:8 is that His people walk humbly with Him. Notice first the word "walk." The question we must first address here is this: What does it mean to walk with God? In Genesis 6, we read about the conditions of the earth in the days of Noah:

(5) The LORD saw that the wickedness of man was great in the earth, and that every intention of the thoughts of his heart was only evil continually. (6) And the LORD regretted that he had made man on the earth, and it grieved him to his heart. (7) So the LORD said, "I will blot out man whom I have created from the face of the land, man and animals and creeping things and birds of the heavens, for I am sorry that I have made them." (8) But Noah found favor in the eyes of the LORD. (9) These are the generations of Noah. Noah was a righteous man, blameless in his generation. Noah walked with God. - Genesis 6:5-9 ESV

The days before the flood were days of tremendous evil. God's heart was grieved because of the rebellion of the people He had created. Notice, however, that one man found favour with God. Genesis 6 describes Noah as "righteous and blameless in his generation" —one who walked with God. Walking with God, according to Genesis 6 implies living in obedience and submission to the authority and purpose of God.

There are two ways we can walk in this life. We can walk with God, or we can walk contrary to Him. Consider the words of God to His people in Leviticus 26:

> 23 *"And if by this discipline you are not turned to me but walk contrary to me, 24 then I also will walk contrary to you, and I myself will strike you sevenfold for your sins. 25 And I will bring a sword upon you, that shall execute vengeance for the covenant. And if you gather within your cities, I will send pestilence among you, and you shall be delivered into the hand of the enemy. - Leviticus 26:23-25 ESV*

Here in this passage, the Lord God rebuked His people for their sins. He had disciplined them because they had disobeyed His commands. He told them that if they persisted in walking contrary to Him, He would bring even greater punishment upon them. Once again, it is clear that walking with God has to do with living in obedience to Him and His purpose for our lives.

1 Samuel 8:1-3 tells us that the sons of Samuel did not walk in God's ways but took bribes and perverted justice:

> 1 *When Samuel became old, he made his sons judges over Israel.   2 The name of his firstborn son was Joel, and the name of his second, Abijah; they were judges in Beersheba. 3 Yet his sons did not walk in his ways but turned aside after gain. They took bribes and perverted justice. - 1 Samuel 8:1-3 ESV*

On the other hand, Jehoshaphat demonstrated that he walked with God by not worshipping the pagan Baals many in Israel worshipped. Instead, he sought the one true God and followed His commandments:

> *3 The LORD was with Jehoshaphat, because he walked in the earlier ways of his father David. He did not seek the Baals, 4 but sought the God of his father and walked in his commandments, and not according to the practices of Israel.*
> *- 2 Chronicles 17:3-4 ESV*

We walk with God when we submit to Him and His purpose. Walking with God implies that we have chosen a particular path in life. That path is a path of righteousness and faithfulness to God, no matter the cost.

Notice also here that we are to walk "humbly" with our God. By choosing to walk with God, we have already submitted to Him and His Lordship. The word "humbly," however, emphasizes what God requires of all who choose to submit to His purpose.

Throughout church history, many have chosen to walk with God but, their motivations and intentions did not come from humility. I would dare say that each of us has had times in our Christian life where our purposes have been less than honourable. I have preached sermons that came from a heart of pride, seeking personal glory. There have been times when I have not submitted to the leading of the Spirit of God. God has revealed sinful attitudes in my heart that I have had to address. I suspect that I am not alone in this.

Many people have chosen to walk with the Lord, but not all walk "humbly" in His presence? A humble walk is what the Lord requires here. What does this humble walk look like? Let's take a moment to see what the Bible has to teach us about humility in our walk with God.

What Does God Require?

Accepting Guilt

Listen to the words of 2 Chronicles 33:23:

> *23 And he did not humble himself before the LORD, as Manasseh his father had humbled himself, but this Amon incurred guilt more and more. - 2 Chronicles 33:23 ESV*

This verse tells us that King Amon did not humble himself before the Lord. This refusal to humble himself was evidenced by his incurring more and more guilt. In other words, King Amon continued in his evil ways and would not repent of his sin. The implication here is that the humble person accepts their guilt and confesses this before God.

2 Kings 22 recounts the story of how King Josiah ordered the cleansing of the temple. During this cleaning, the Book of the Law was discovered. When Shaphan, the secretary, read the book, he had it brought to King Josiah. After the words were read to Josiah, he tore his clothes in a sign of humility and despair. He realized that, as a people, they had disobeyed this Law. He sent his servants immediately to a prophetess to hear from the Lord about this matter. Listen to the words of the prophetess Huldah:

> *18 But to the king of Judah, who sent you to inquire of the LORD, thus shall you say to him, Thus says the LORD, the God of Israel: Regarding the words that you have heard, 19 because your heart was penitent, and you humbled yourself before the LORD, when you heard how I spoke against this place and against its inhabitants, that they should become a desolation and a curse, and you have torn your clothes and wept before me, I also have heard you, declares the LORD. - 2 Kings 22:18-19 ESV*

Walking Humbly With God

Huldah told Josiah that God would show mercy in his day because he humbled himself by demonstrating a penitent heart. Josiah's humility was demonstrated by how his heart was broken when he discovered that he had been disobedient to the purpose of God. The king took steps to correct his disobedience. He submitted to the Law of God and did all he could to walk in step with it. Walking humbly with God requires recognition of guilt and a willingness to repent and correct our ways.

Surrendering to God's Purpose

When Moses went to Pharaoh to request that he let the Israelites God, Pharaoh refused. Moses made it clear to him that it was the purpose of God that His people leave, but Pharaoh would have nothing to do with it. A series of plagues were unleashed on Egypt, confirming that God was behind the request of Moses. These plagues made it very hard for Pharaoh not to see that God was in this request. Notice, however, the words of Moses to Pharaoh in Exodus 10:3:

3 So Moses and Aaron went in to Pharaoh and said to him, "Thus says the LORD, the God of the Hebrews, 'How long will you refuse to humble yourself before me? Let my people go, that they may serve me. - Exodus 10:3 ESV

Moses asked Pharaoh how long he would refuse to humble himself before God. Pharaoh dug in and rebelled against the purpose of God. Consider, however, what it meant for Pharaoh to surrender to God's purpose. He would lose a great number of slaves. These slaves built his cities and provided free labour for Him. How would he replace well over a million slaves? What would be the economic impact of these slaves being freed? There was a high price tag attached to this request of God. The cost was just too much for Pharaoh.

I have met families who have, sold their homes and left their country to be obedient to the call of God in their lives. I have met young men who have chosen to abandon their old friends because of their negative influence on their spiritual lives. I have met young women who have endured hardship at the hands of their own families because they turned from their family religion to follow the Lord Jesus. These individuals humbled themselves before God and surrendered their possessions, reputations and relationships to walk with Him. Walking humbly before God will require a willingness to lay everything at His feet in surrender, no matter the cost.

Being an Instrument of Compassion

Isaiah spoke to his people about their practice of fasting. These individuals put on sackcloth, covered themselves with ashes and walked about with their heads bowed. The Lord God, however, asked His people to consider if this was the kind of humility He required:

> *5 Is such the fast that I choose, a day for a person to humble himself? Is it to bow down his head like a reed, and to spread sackcloth and ashes under him? Will you call this a fast, and a day acceptable to the LORD? – Isaiah 58:5 ESV*

Isaiah explains that true humility was not about not eating, wearing uncomfortable clothes and walking about with a sombre attitude. Instead, the humbling God required ministering to those in need:

6 "Is not this the fast that I choose: to loose the bonds of wickedness, to undo the straps of the yoke, to let the oppressed go free, and to break every yoke? 7 Is it not to share your bread with the hungry and bring the homeless poor into your house; when you see the naked, to cover him, and not to hide yourself from your own flesh? - Isaiah 58:6-7 ESV

True humility, according to God, was to undo the yoke, release the captives, and share your bread with the hungry. It involved bringing the homeless into your home and clothing the naked. The humble person is an instrument of compassion—the humble reach out to those who are more needy and ease their pain. To walk humbly with God requires a compassionate heart and willing heart to make a change in the lives of those who are oppressed.

Recognition of Need

Where does the strength come from to be humble? Our natural tendency is to think of ourselves and our own needs. We give reluctantly. The humble person understands the source of their strength and taps into it. Consider what Ezra did when he was charged to return to Israel to help in its reconstruction:

21 Then I proclaimed a fast there, at the river Ahava, that we might humble ourselves before our God, to seek from him a safe journey for ourselves, our children, and all our goods. 22 For I was ashamed to ask the king for a band of soldiers and horsemen to protect us against the enemy on our way, since we had told the king, "The hand of our God is for good on all who seek him, and the power of his wrath is against all who forsake him." 23 So we fasted and implored

71

What Does God Require?

our God for this, and he listened to our entreaty. - Ezra 8:21-23 ESV

Knowing the immensity of the task before him, Ezra proclaimed a fast at the Ahava River. That day they implored God for wisdom and protection for the responsibility before them. They understood their need for God to accomplish the task. They understood that there would be opposition and that unless God protected them, they would surely fail. Ezra did not trust his ability and wisdom. Instead, he confessed his weakness and need to God. That day he chose to look to His Creator for the strength necessary to accomplish the task. It is the proud person who relies on their own strength. The proud do not see their need for God's support and equipping. They count on their experience, education and skill to do the task.

The humble, however, cast themselves on God. They implore Hm for the strength, wisdom and provision they need. If you are going to walk humbly with God, you will need to recognize that your strength and wisdom are insufficient. You will need to draw deeply from Him and what He alone can provide to live and serve Him as He requires. The sin of your heart cannot be conquered in the strength of the flesh. You cannot save a single soul –this is the work of God's Spirit. God does not work according to human wisdom. His ways are often very different from ours. If you are going to accomplish the task He has given you, you will need to confess your need of His wisdom, leading and enabling. You will need to stop leaning on your understanding and trust in His (see Proverbs 3:5-6).

Will you allow God to expose sin in your life? Will you confess that sin and repent of it? Are you willing to lay everything down in surrender to the Lord today? Will you submit to His lordship? Will you offer yourself as an instrument of compassion? Will you look to Him alone for wisdom, strength and provision? If so, you are beginning to understand what it means to walk humbly with God.

For Prayer:

Lord God, you are the definition of holiness. We confess that as we stand before you, we have fallen short of Your standard. We ask that You search our hearts and reveal any sin in us. Give us the humility to confess our sin. Give us a heart to surrender all to you today. We acknowledge that there are things in our lives that we don't want you to touch. We abandon them to you. We pray that you move us out as a surrendered people to minister compassionately to those around us in Your name. Forgive us for believing that the kingdom of God depends on human strength and wisdom. Please help us to recognize our weaknesses. Teach us to know and follow Your leading. Show us the difference between human wisdom and the wisdom of God. Show us how to rely less on our strength and to trust more in You. Give us the grace to walk humbly with You each day.

Light To My Path Book Distribution

Light To My Path Book Distribution (LTMP) is a book writing and distribution ministry reaching out to needy Christian workers in Asia, Latin America, and Africa. Many Christian workers in developing countries do not have the resources necessary to obtain Bible training or purchase Bible study materials for their ministries and personal encouragement. F. Wayne Mac Leod is a member of Action International Ministries and has been writing these books with a goal to distribute them freely or at cost price to needy pastors and Christian workers around the world.

Tens of thousands of these books have been distributed and used in preaching, teaching, evangelism and encouragement of local believers in over sixty countries. Books are now being translated into a variety of languages. The goal is to make them available to as many believers as possible.

The ministry of LTMP is a faith-based ministry, and we trust the Lord for the resources necessary to distribute the books for the encouragement and strengthening of believers around the world. Would you pray that the Lord would open doors for the translation and further distribution of these books?

For more information about Light To My Path visit our website at www.lighttomypath.ca

Printed in Great Britain
by Amazon